# TENPIN
# BOWLING

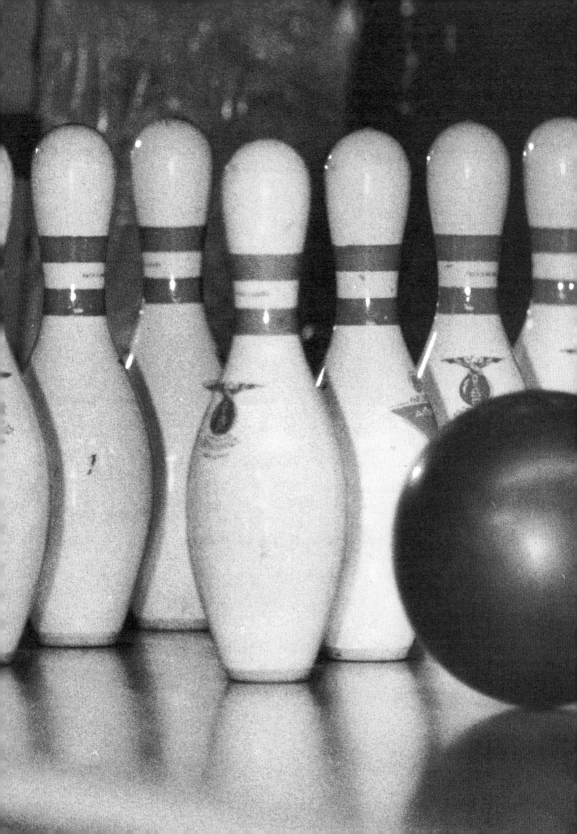

# PLAY·THE·GAME

# TENPIN BOWLING

Henry Harrison ·

Ward Lock Limited · London

First published in Great Britain in 1988
by Ward Lock Limited, 8 Clifford Street
London W1X 1RB, an Egmont Company

Series Editor Ian Morrison
Designed by Anita Ruddell
Figure drawings by Tony Randell
Other illustrations by Ian Foulis

Text set in Helvetica
by Hourds Typographica, Stafford, England
Printed and bound in Great Britain
by Richard Clay Ltd, Bungay, Suffolk

**British Library Cataloguing in Publication Data**
Harrison, Henry
    Tenpin bowling.——(Play the game (Ward
    Lock (Firm))2.
    1. Bowling
    I. Title    II. Series
    794.6        GV903

    ISBN 0-7063-6659-X

# *Acknowledgments*

The author and publishers would like to
thank Maurice Glazer, MBE, General
Secretary of the British Tenpin Bowling
Association, for his help in the preparation
of this book.

Thanks are also due to Colorsport, who
supplied the photographs reproduced on
pages 2, 19, 43, 49 and 58.

*Frontispiece:* **A strike in the offing?**

# CONTENTS

# FOREWORD

Tenpin bowling is, without a doubt, one of the most exciting of all games to play; the extreme accuracy needed to make strikes and spares makes it equally as skilful. All sports have their great achievements: in darts it is the 180 throw; in snooker it is the 147 break; and in tenpin bowling it is that magical 300 game. It has been said that it is more difficult to score a 300 game in tenpin bowling than it is to score a hole-in-one in golf. Only accuracy will give you a 300 game in bowling, but even the most skilful golfer needs a big slice of luck to make a hole-in-one.

For reasons best known to anthropologists, it is apparently perfectly natural for human beings to want to throw objects at one another. This may account for the reasoning in some circles that the headpin in bowling replaces the object of one's anger or tension – that is, an objectionable person!

To the casual bowler, one who plays the game as a hobby rather than competitively, the way in which inhibitions may be cast off on a set of tenpins can create great enjoyment. Although a similar feeling may be experienced by the more serious and competitive player, the aggression now changes to 'killer instinct'. However, no matter whether you play for fun, to get rid of your aggression, or whether you play to the highest level, tenpin bowling will always offer great pleasure for both the beginner and the expert.

In the course of many years, only a few books have been published about the game. They have ranged from handbooks containing very simplified facts to highly specialized volumes. But *Play the Game: Tenpin Bowling* offers a comprehensive general outline, covering the whole field of the game as it is played today, in one slim, handy volume.

Those of you taking the sport up for the first time will have no problems coming to a quick understanding of the game with this indispensable book. For those of you who already have a basic knowledge, *Play the Game: Tenpin Bowling* will help you develop your existing skills. It is my belief that the information in these pages, clearly written in precise and simple terms, will serve to dispel any mystery that the game may hold for some people. There is no doubt in my mind that *Play the Game: Tenpin Bowling* will provide thousands of readers with the rudiments of knowledge of the game and assist with developing the power of concentration needed for greater achievement.

**Maurice Glazer MBE**
*General Secretary of the*
*British Tenpin Bowling Association*

# FOREWORD

# HISTORY & DEVELOPMENT OF BOWLING

**B**owling, in one form or another, must be regarded as one of man's oldest pastimes. Objects for use in a game similar to bowling have been found in an Egyptian child's tomb dating to 5200BC. A game known as *Bocci*, and resembling bowling, was played in what is now northern Italy around 50BC. The Polynesians were known to have played *Ula Maika*, a game similar to bowling which used small elliptical balls and flat round stones. By coincidence they used to roll their ball a distance of 60ft (18·3m), which is the same distance used in modern-day tenpin bowling.

The use of bowling 'pins', however, can be traced to Germany in the third or fourth century, when local peasants would set up clubs, known as *kegels*, in the cloisters of churches and throw large round stones at them. The *kegels* represented *Heide* (the heathen one) and the game had more significance than obtaining strikes and spares as in today's game; if you hit a *kegel* you were said to be free from sin, but if you missed you had to indulge in extra prayer . . .

Priests themselves started playing the game, and Martin Luther's liking of the game made it very popular at the time of the Reformation. Luther is believed to have been responsible for standardizing the number of pins at nine and for drawing up the first set of rules. There exists a Nine Pin Bowling Association today and their headquarters are, coincidentally, in West Germany.

The game eventually spread to England, but Edward III, intent on spoiling everybody's fun in those days, banned the game (just as he did with other leisurely pursuits) because it interfered with archery practice. However, because of its simplicity, the game remained popular and survived. Henry VIII was less miserable than Edward, and he even built alleys at Whitehall. The game became very popular, particularly at fairs. The number of 'pins' varied from three up to as many as fifteen. The weight of the ball also varied considerably; some were made of wood while sometimes cannon balls were used! And of course, local conditions dictated the length of the 'alley'.

The popularity of bowling attracted many gamblers, and Henry VIII eventually banned the game because it ceased to be a sport and became more a means of making illicit money (see, he *was* just as miserable as Edward after all!).

# HISTORY · & · DEVELOPMENT

Bowling with ten pins laid out in triangular formation was believed to have first been played at Suffolk, England in 1803. But the development of the sport as we know it today can be attributed to Dutch migrants, who took the game of nine pins to the United States when they settled at New Amsterdam (now New York) in 1626. By the mid-nineteenth century the game was flourishing, particularly in New York City, as alleys sprung up on most street corners. Its popularity and rapid growth attracted a great deal of gambling and eventually the game was taken over by hoodlums and gangsters. Consequently nine pins was banned as state after state followed Connecticut's banning of the game in 1841.

There was only one way around the law – add another pin and call it ten pins! It worked, and since then the sport has developed into one of the biggest indoor pastimes in the United States. Naturally, size of alleys (lanes as they are now called), balls and pins varied from state to state. Even today other varieties of bowling are played, notably with smaller pins than in the conventional tenpin game. The most popular is duckpin bowling, played with smaller pins (approx. $9\frac{1}{2}$in (24cm) high) and with a 5in (12·5cm) diameter ball, but with no holes drilled in it. It is played predominantly in the New England states and along the eastern coast of America. A Duck Pin Association has existed since 1927.

The first attempt to form a national association in 1875 (the National Bowling League) was unsuccessful. Fifteen years later an attempt to form the American Bowling Union also met with failure.

The American Bowling Congress (ABC) was, however, formed following a meeting at the Beethoven Hall, New York, in September 1895, and it became responsible for standardizing the rules and the control of the game in general. A lot of credit for the game's early development as an organized sport must go to Elmer H. Baumgarten, the president and executive secretary of the ABC

**The duckpin**

*Duckpins are still popular in the United States. The duckpin (on the right) is considerably smaller than the conventional tenpin.*

for many years.

Predominantly a male domain in the early part of the twentieth century, women gradually took to the game and in 1916 the Women's International Bowling Congress was formed in St Louis. Boys and girls also played the game in their thousands and in 1935 the American Junior Bowling Congress (AJBC) was formed.

Despite its ever-increasing popularity as a

pastime, it was only with the development of the automatic pinspotter by AMF International in 1951 that the game turned from being a pastime into a major international sport.

Pin boys had previously been employed to reset knocked-down pins, but that was time consuming. Now, the game was speeded up and new plush indoor bowling centres were erected throughout the United States. The bowling centre was no longer a dingy place but a bright, comfortable hall where the whole family could spend many hours either playing or watching the sport.

The automatic pinspotter was introduced to many other countries, including Great Britain in 1960. After many meetings and discussions the British Tenpin Bowling Association (BTBA) was formed in May 1961 and became affiliated to the sport's governing body, the Fédération Internationale des Quilleurs (FIQ), which was formed in 1954. The ABC also became affiliated to the FIQ the same year.

From its humble beginnings membership of the BTBA grew from a few hundred to thirty thousand within five years. Bowling in Britain declined in the late sixties and the bowling centres made way for the less strenuous activity of Bingo. Happily the sport is increasing in popularity once more.

At its peak in the 1960s there were 125 bowling centres in Britain with 2,500 lanes; the BTBA had 34,000 members. In 1987, although the number of centres was only 70 providing 1,000 lanes, membership of the association was higher at 40,000. Tenpin bowling is more popular than it was in the 1960s, and consequently more lanes are being created up and down Great Britain to cope with the anticipated 'second' boom.

These figures, however, pale into insignificance when one considers there are something like 5 million members of the ABC, $4\frac{1}{2}$ million members of the WIBC and approximately 1 million members of the AJBC in the United States. In addition, millions play the game on a casual basis and do not belong to a league.

It is estimated that more than 70 million people play the game in the United States alone, and nearly 80 million worldwide in approximately 100 countries. Many bowling centres have in excess of 100 lanes, particularly in the United States and Japan. The largest in Europe is the Nottingham Bowl with 48 lanes.

The United States is the obvious stronghold of the sport and it is estimated there are approximately 9,000 bowling establishments, including the White House. There are around 2,000 professional players in the United States who belong to the Professional Bowlers Association (PBA) which was formed in 1958. The association organizes sponsored season-long events for its members, and top players can win anything up to $250,000 in a season. There is also a Women's Professional Bowlers Association in the United States; it was founded in 1978 and has approximately 275 members.

World amateur championships have been held since 1923 and were originally organized under the auspices of the International Bowling Association. Since 1954, however, the FIQ has organized the championships; the first being at Helsinki, Finland in 1954. They are currently held every four years, for both men and women, and the next will be in 1991.

Tenpin bowling is an easy game to play, and is one of those games that can be played purely for fun. It does not have to be played competitively to get the fullest enjoyment out of it. The one thing that bowling has in its favour is the warm and friendly environment of the bowling centre. It is an ideal place for the whole family. There are not many sports than can boast such a claim these days. Tenpin bowling is one of the most popular participant sports in the world – you only need to play the game once to find out why. In fact, chances are that you will soon become hooked and will pay regular visits to your local bowling centre!

# EQUIPMENT & TERMINOLOGY

**B**efore you play your first game of tenpin bowling, it will do you no harm to familiarize yourself with the equipment used and the terminology you will encounter.

First of all we will look at the equipment required to play a game.

*The ball*

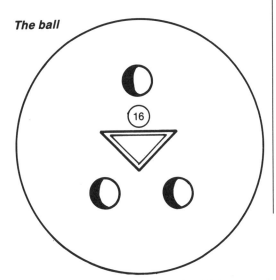

*The standard bowling ball. It should have a circumference of 27in (68·58cm) and weigh no more than 16lb (13·26kg). The thumb hole is shown at the top and the two finger holes are below the centre of the ball.*

## *EQUIPMENT*

The advantage of taking up tenpin bowling is that you do not need to purchase any equipment to play. All equipment can be hired from your local bowling centre.

Essentially, all you need is ten pins and a ball. But the modern indoor game is more sophisticated than that. It is played on a smoothly polished wooden surface and mechanical pinspotters mean you can concentrate on your game while the pins are being re-spotted for you. The only other equipment you need is proper footwear and sensible clothing.

Let's look at each item in turn.

### The ball

The ball is made of very hard rubber, plastic, or composition material. Early balls were made of *Lignum vitae*, a very hard wood that was also used in the manufacture of lawn bowls. The early bowling balls had no

*This is a standard tennis ball, drawn to scale to demonstrate the size of the bowling ball.*

finger holes in them and had a tendency to crack, chip, or even warp. Finger holes appeared in the early part of the twentieth century and in 1905 the first hard rubber balls were produced, thus ending the life of the wooden ball.

The original rubber balls were red, but black soon became the adopted colour by the ABC. However, with the introduction of plastic balls in the 1960s, coloured mottled balls became the vogue and are still popular today.

The circumference of a bowling ball is 27in (68·58cm), and its weight varies depending upon personal preference. The lightest balls are normally 8lb (6·63kg) for children, up to a maximum 16lb (13·26kg) for adults.

Each ball has three holes drilled into it. Leading professional players often have balls with five holes to enable them to play with their middle fingers in different positions according to the shot. One is to accommodate the thumb and the other two for your middle two fingers and *not* your index and middle finger as some beginners often believe.

It is important that you have the correct weight of ball and that your thumb and fingers fit properly. If they don't you will have all sorts of problems when you come to delivering your first ball. The correct procedure for finding the right ball can be found on page 48.

All bowling centres have a selection of balls available for your use, and a little time spent searching among the racks for one that is suited to your needs will make your game a lot easier and more comfortable. If your thumb starts hurting after delivering a few balls then you have obviously selected one with the wrong sized holes.

If you decide that you want to play the game seriously and regularly, you are well advised to invest in your own ball. The cost is around £60 to £100, but it is money well spent because many of the balls available for use at your local bowling centre will be

*The pin*

15 in
(38.1 cm)

*The standard pin should be 15in (38·1cm) tall and weigh no more than 3lb 10oz (1·64kg) if made of wood, or 3lb 6oz (1·53kg) if made out of a synthetic material.*

chipped as a result of constant use. Don't forget, if you do buy your own ball you will need a bag to put it in . . . just try getting on a crowded bus carrying a bowling ball!

The choice of weight is very important. A

**The ten pins standing in position, their spot number indicated on the scoreboard above.**

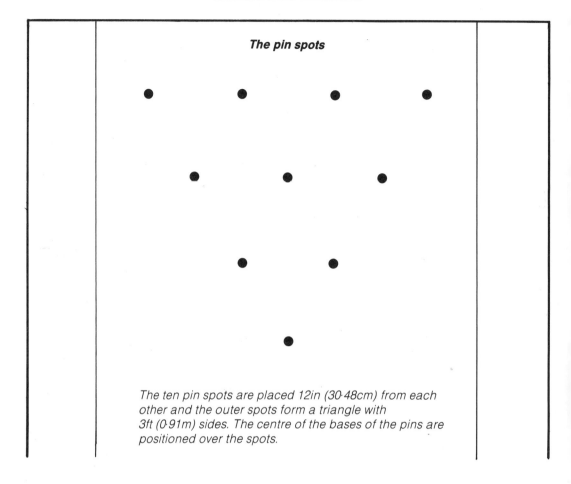

*The pin spots*

*The ten pin spots are placed 12in (30·48cm) from each other and the outer spots form a triangle with 3ft (0·91m) sides. The centre of the bases of the pins are positioned over the spots.*

heavier ball will knock down more pins, but if you are using too heavy a ball you will lose a lot of accuracy.

## The pins

Since the ABC adopted its first set of rules the size of pins has varied little. The first pins were made of a solid piece of maple, but they are now made of six strips of maple stuck together, shaped and coated in plastic.

There are, as the name implies, ten pins. Each must be the same size and weight. They are shaped and stand 15in (38·1cm) tall. They must weigh between 3lb 6oz and 3lb 10oz (1·53–1·64kg).

The pins are placed on spots equidistant from each other, and within a triangle whose sides measure 3ft (0·91m). The distance between the centre of each pin to the adjacent pin is 12in (30·48cm). The pins do not have numbers marked on them but each pin is referred to by a number according to its position within the triangle.

*Above right: The pins do not have numbers marked on them but are referred to by a number according to their pin position.*

*Below right: This is how the pins look when spotted. The numbers are for identification purposes only.*

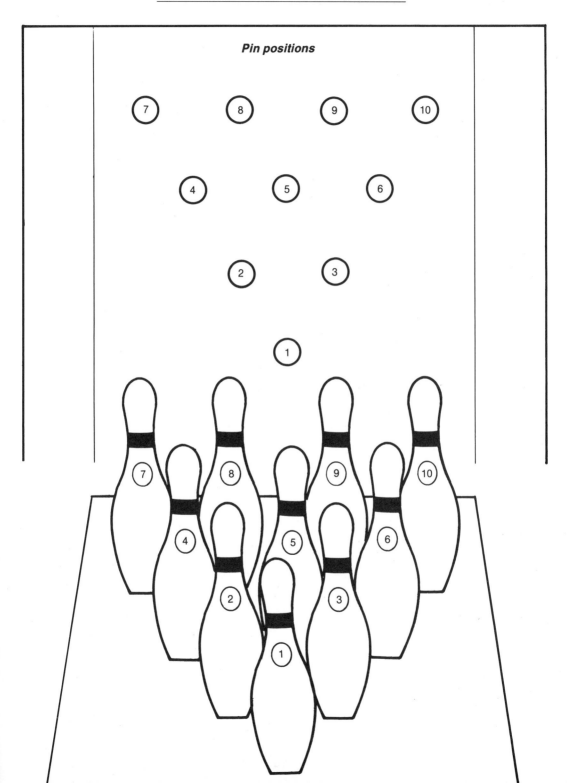

*Pin positions*

## The lane

Bowling centres vary in size. A centre may have at least two lanes or it can have in excess of 100. The average bowling centre in Britain has around twenty lanes. As each lane requires something like 100ft( 30m) to accommodate the run-up, playing area and maintenance area, a large floor area is required to set up even the smallest of bowling centres.

Each lane is constructed of thin strips of maple and pine wood, although many modern lanes are now made out of laminated plastic. They are very smooth, and are varnished, polished and coated with a thin layer of oil, known as the 'lane dressing'. The dressing must not extend further than 26ft (7·92m) beyond the foul line. A ball delivered on the oiled area slides across the lane, but once it makes contact with the dry area, it starts to spin. The lanes are oiled every day. The lane is 42in (1·07m) wide and a foul line drawn across the width indicates the point which you must not cross either before or after delivering your ball. An electronic eye passes across the lane at the foul line and indicates if the foot has passed over the foul line either during or after delivery.

The length of the lane is measured from the foul line to the head pin (the pin at the apex of the triangle) and is 60ft (18·29m). Alongside each lane, from the foul line to the end of the lane, is a gutter to catch any

*The foul line*

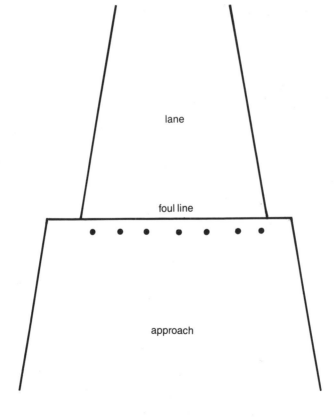

lane

foul line

approach

## The lane

The distance from the head pin (no 1 pin) to the foul line is 60ft (18·29m).

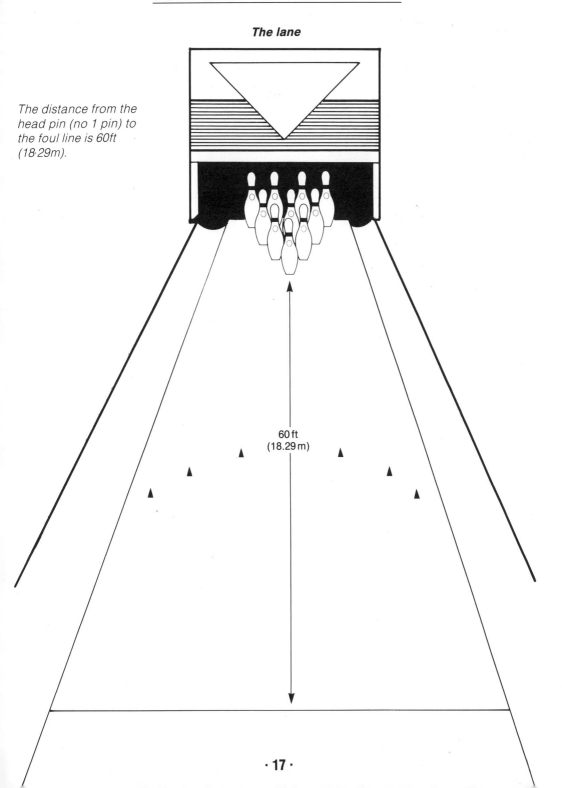

60 ft
(18.29 m)

**The gutter**

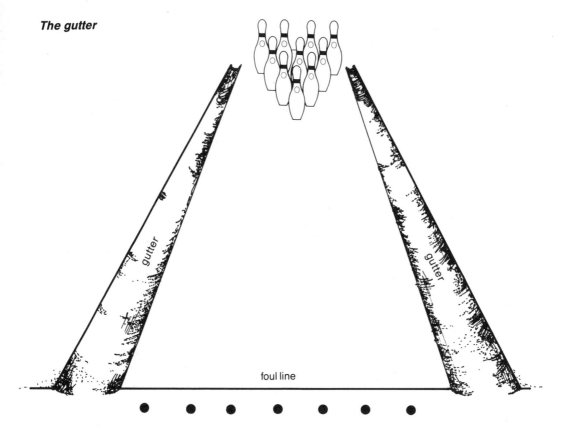

foul line

*The gutter extends from the foul line the length of the lane. Its width is slightly greater than the diameter of the ball and will cause all wayward balls to make their way direct to the pinspotter.*

wayward balls. The gutter is approximately 4in (10·16cm) deep and 9in (22·85cm) wide. Any balls that end up in the gutter are recycled through the machinery and returned to you. If your first ball goes in the gutter don't think that you can send your second ball down the lane straight away – you cannot. The pinspotter has still got to go through the action of re-setting the pins. Just because you didn't knock any pins down it doesn't mean the pinspotter can have a bit of relaxation!

All lanes have a set of guide marks at a point approximately 7–12ft (2·13–3·64m) from the foul line. These markers, which consist of seven arrow-shaped pointers, are very important, and a good bowler will use them to their fullest in perfecting his play. For the full explanation of their purpose and how to use them, see the Technique section (page 48).

There should be a run-up (called the approach) of at least 15ft (4·60m) before the foul line. There are two very important sets of markers on the approach. These are to guide you in positioning your feet as you take up your stance. For details of their use and importance see pages 57–62.

A Belgian competitor delivers a ball during a ladies match at the World Games.

## Guide marks

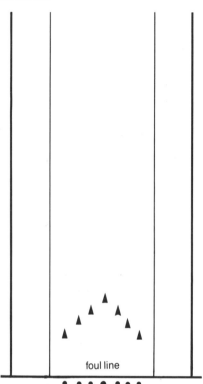

foul line

The guide marks are a useful aid to accurate bowling.

## The pinspotter

It is only since the invention of the automatic pinspotter by the AMF Company in 1951 that bowling became as popular as it is today in the United States. At one time your ball had to be recovered by hand and the pins removed and re-spotted manually. But with the advent of the automatic pinspotter, it is all done for you after each delivery.

After your first ball a bar will drop on to the lane. All pins left standing will be picked up by the pinspotter and pins knocked down will be swept away to the back of the machinery. The pins still standing are then automatically replaced on their correct spots. After your second roll (assuming you did not knock all ten pins down with your first roll) the machine will remove all pins, whether standing or knocked down, and re-spot *all* ten for the next player's turn. It is important not to deliver a ball until the pinspotter has completed its operations, as it can damage the machinery and, just as importantly, cause you to forfeit a ball during your game.

In addition to removing and replacing pins, the pinspotter makes a note via its

The automatic pinsetter has revolutionized the game of tenpin bowling.

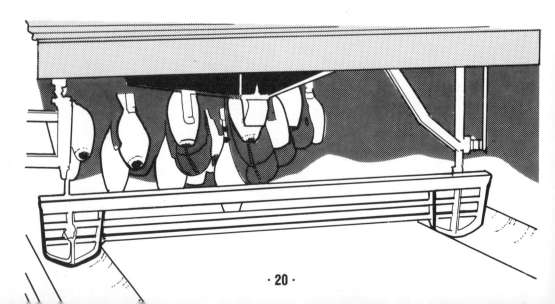

*Electronic pin indicator*

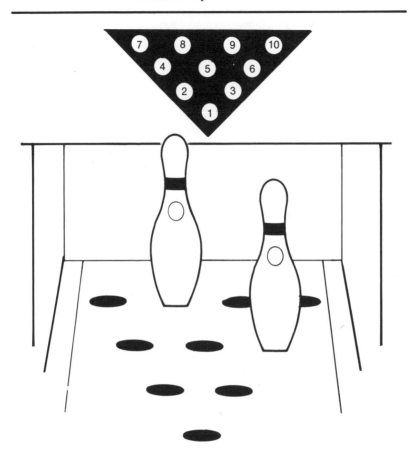

*The electronic pin indicator will display the numbered pins picked up by the pinspotter by illuminating the numbers.*

electronic brain, which pins it has picked up in the process of re-spotting. On some machines that information is passed on to you by means of an electronic indicator positioned above the lane. That way you can see clearly how many pins have been knocked down with your first ball. It does not display the number of pins knocked down with the second ball however, and you must be ready to count the number of pins left standing (if any) after your second delivery.

The electronic indicator will also advise if you made a strike by displaying a large X.

To demonstrate its versatility even further, the pinspotter automatically returns your ball via a track (known as the return) that is situated between your lane and the adjacent one. Many lanes have underlane ball returns these days. Make sure you pick up the right ball and not one being used by somebody else, and don't pick your ball up while the person on the adjacent line is about to play.

*Bowling shoes*

When collecting your ball from the delivery ramp be careful where you position your hand because another ball could be on its way back and cause you a nasty injury!

## Footwear

Shoes can be hired, at a small cost, from most bowling centres, but once more it is worth investing in a pair of your own if you intend playing regularly. The cost is in the region of £20 to £25. When you hire a pair of shoes, the attendant will take your own shoes in exchange, which will be returned when you return the bowling shoes.

Bowling shoes are so designed as to let you start and stop your run-up correctly. They have leather soles, to enable you to slide, and rubber heels to enable you to stop.

Whatever you do you **must not play in ordinary shoes**. They can severely damage the lane. Furthermore you are likely to be ejected from your bowling centre if you do.

## Clothing

There are no rules for the wearing of clothing but commonsense will tell you not to wear tight-fitting shirts or blouses. The looser they are, the more freedom of movement you will have. That also applies to trousers and tight skirts.

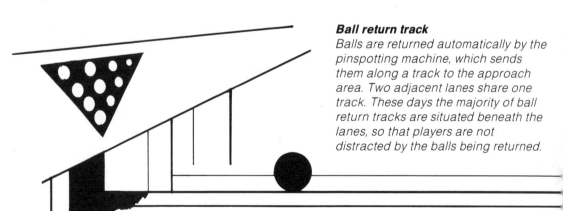

*Ball return track*
*Balls are returned automatically by the pinspotting machine, which sends them along a track to the approach area. Two adjacent lanes share one track. These days the majority of ball return tracks are situated beneath the lanes, so that players are not distracted by the balls being returned.*

## Other accessories

Some bowlers like to wear a wrist support to give extra strength to their wrist. Some wrist supports are extended to provide support to the base of the thumb. It is important to keep your hands from getting sticky, and you will find a fresh air vent near the ball return at the end of the lane for this purpose.

Someone has to score a game, whether it be the players in turn, or an independent scorer. He or she is provided with a table and chair at the end of the lane. Under match conditions, a light above the table is illuminated and this, via a magnifier, magnifies the score sheet and displays it on a large illuminated screen above the lane. More sophisticated and modern centres have computerized scorers linked to the pinspotter. All you have to do is key in your name, and the computer does the rest . . . well not quite, you still have to knock the pins down!

Right, that is tenpin bowling equipment – now a look at some of the many terms and expressions you will come up against and soon find yourself using.

# TERMINOLOGY

**Alley** Another name for the lane.

**Approach** The run-up area behind the foul line.

**Arrows** The name given to the seven markers on the lane just in front of the foul line.

**Baby split** A split involving the 2 and 7 or the 3 and 10 pins.

*Baby split*

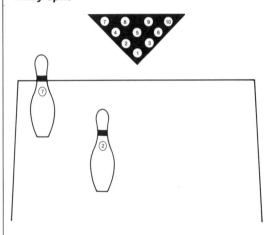

*This is the 2-7 'baby split'. Another example of the baby split is the 3-6.*

**Back-up ball** A ball that curves to the right for a right-handed bowler is known as a back-up bowl. It curves to the left for the left-handed bowler.

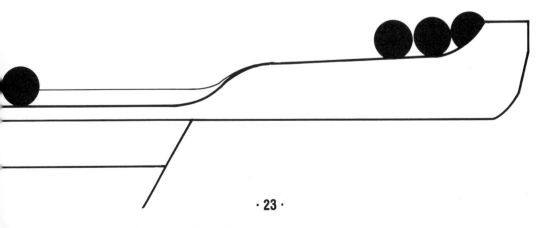

## Back-up ball

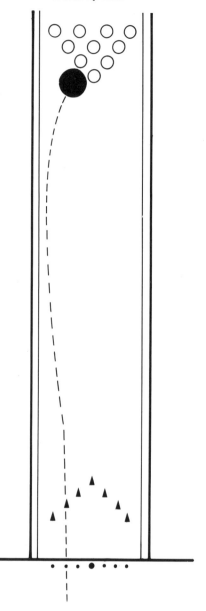

**Bed posts**   The split involving the 4 and 6 or 7 and 10 pins.

**Beer frame**   When a player has a score of 111 at the end of the seventh frame, it is known as the 'beer frame'. It is so called because you have to buy your fellow players a drink!

**Big four**   The 4-6-7-10 split is known as the 'big four'.

**Blow**   See **Error**.

**Bonus**   The additional pins added to your score for getting a strike or spare.

**Brooklyn**   When a right-handed player makes a strike by causing his bowl to hit the left-hand side of the head pin (or vice versa for a left-handed bowler).

**Bucket**   When four pins in a cluster are left after the first roll they are known as a 'bucket', The 1-2-3-5, 2-4-5-8 and 3-5-6-9 leaves are examples of buckets.

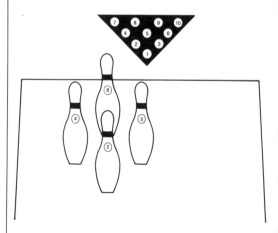

*The back-up ball played by the right-hander is played down the left side of the lane with the ball curving towards the 1-2 pocket. This delivery is well worth mastering early on.*

**Bucket**

*Four pins left in a cluster are described as a 'bucket'. The 3-5-6-9 leave is also a 'bucket', and so is the 1-2-3-5 leave.*

# EQUIPMENT · & · TERMINOLOGY

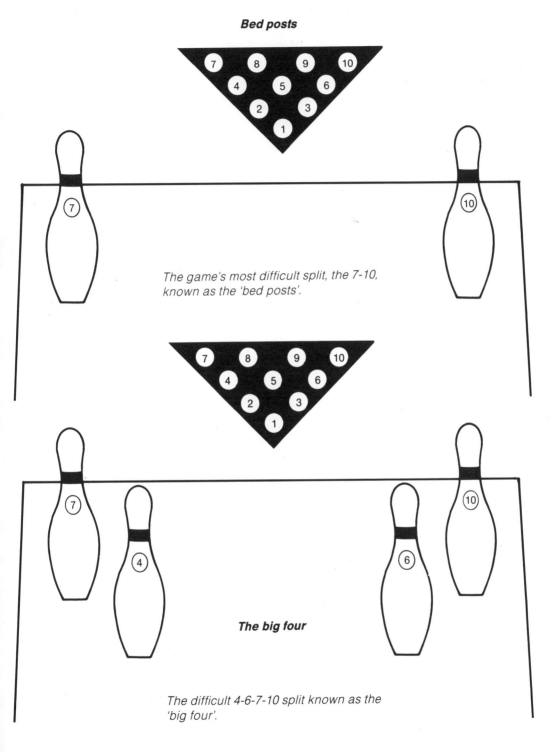

***Bed posts***

*The game's most difficult split, the 7-10, known as the 'bed posts'.*

***The big four***

*The difficult 4-6-7-10 split known as the 'big four'.*

# TENPIN · BOWLING

## The clothes line

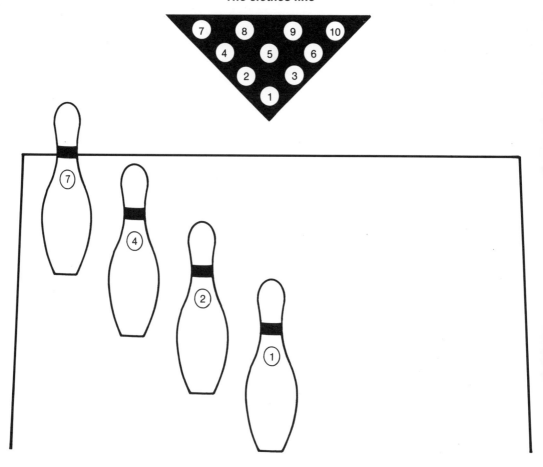

The leaving of four pins in a row is called a 'clothes line'
or a 'fence'. The 1-3-6-10 leave is another 'clothes line'.

**Cherry**   When the ball knocks down a single pin when attempting a spare consisting of more than one pin.

**Clothes line**   The leave containing either the 1-2-4-7 or 1-3-6-10 pins. It is also known as the 'fence'.

**Creeper**   A slowly-rolled ball.

**Crossover**   Another name for the Brooklyn.

**Curve**   A ball that starts off on the right-hand side of the lane and curves in towards the centre is called a curve. This applies to right-handed bowlers; it is the opposite for left-handed players.

**Dead mark**   A 'dead mark' is when you make a strike or spare on the very last ball of the tenth frame. No bonus is scored for a dead mark, but of course you will never do yourself any harm by playing one.

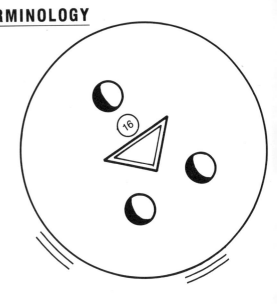

### Curve

*The curve ball starts off on the right and curves in towards the 1-3 pocket (vice versa for left-handed players).*

**Delivery** The rolling of the ball towards the pins is known as a delivery. It is also called a roll.

**Double** Two strikes in succession from one bowler.

**Dutchman** A game in which a player alternates between strikes and spares in each frame to give a score of 200.

### Dutchman

*The scorecard for a 'Dutchman 200' game, involving alternate strikes and spares, could well look something like this.*

| 1 | 2 | 3 | 4 | 5 | 6 | 7 | 8 | 9 | 10 | Total |
|---|---|---|---|---|---|---|---|---|---|---|
| ☒ | 7 ☒ | ☒ | 8 / | ☒ | 9 / | ☒ | 9 / | ☒ | 8 / ☒ | |
| 20 | 40 | 60 | 80 | 100 | 120 | 140 | 160 | 180 | 200 | 200 |

## High hit

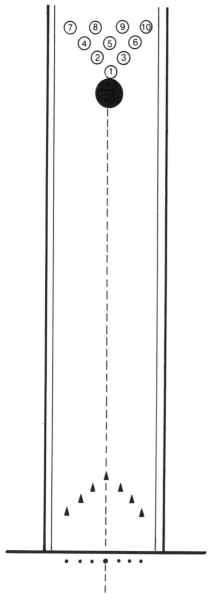

*If you hit the head pin full on your ball will travel through the pins, deflecting the 2-3 pins, taking the 5-8-9 pins and possibly the 7 and 10 pins by deflection. Pins 4 and 6 will almost certainly remain standing.*

**Error** A player is said to have made an error if he fails to get a strike or spare in a frame, but not when the spare involves a split.

**Fence** A row of pins standing after the first roll is called a fence. The 1-2-4-7 leave is known as the left fence while the 1-3-6-10 leave is the right fence. Also known as the 'clothes line'.

**Foul line** The foul line is drawn across the lane at a point 60ft (18·29m) from the head pin.

**Frame** A frame constitutes two rolls of the ball. If you knock all ten pins down with your first roll then the frame is completed.

**Game** A game consists of ten frames.

**Gutter ball** A ball that goes into the gutter before making contact with a pin.

**Head pin** The pin at the apex of the triangle of pins (the number one pin).

**High hit** A ball that hits the head pin full on is called a 'high hit'. The 4-6 or 4-6-7-10 split is likely to result after a high hit (also known as a 'nose hit').

**Hook** A 'hook' is a ball that travels in a straight line either on the right or left of the centre of the lane (depending upon whether you are right- or left-handed) but then curves sharply towards the centre of the lane.

**Kegler** Another name given to a bowler. It stems from the early Germans who used to play with a *kegel*.

**King pin** The Number 5 pin is known as the 'king pin'.

**Lane** The wooden area between the foul line and the back of the pin deck.

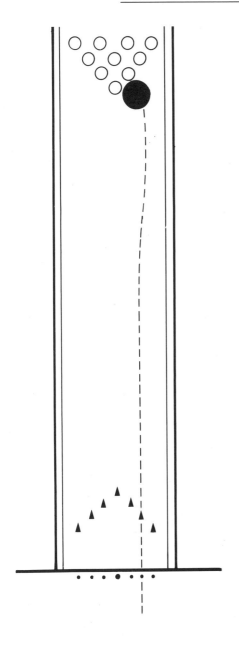

### Hook

*The hook: for right-handed bowlers the ball travels straight before curving left towards the 1-3 pocket (vice versa for left-handed bowlers). The hook is the most effective shot in bowling.*

**Leave**   The number of pins left standing after the delivery of the first ball.

**Line**   Another name for a game.

**Lofting**   'Lofting' occurs when the ball is released too late and is 'dropped' onto the lane rather than rolled on to it. Lofting generally occurs if the holes in the ball are the wrong size for your fingers or thumb. Lofting can seriously damage the lane.

**Miss**   See **Error**.

**Mixer**   A ball which causes the pins to mix together and spin, causing other pins to be knocked down, is call a 'mixer'.

**Nose hit**   See **High hit**.

**Open frame**   A frame in which neither a strike nor a spare is made.

**Perfect game**   The scoring of 12 consecutive strikes in one game will result in the 'perfect game' with the maximum score of 300.

### The perfect game

*If ever you score a perfect game (12 strikes), this is what your scorecard will look like.*

| | 1 | 2 | 3 | 4 | 5 | 6 | 7 | 8 | 9 | 10 | Total |
|---|---|---|---|---|---|---|---|---|---|---|---|
| ⊠ | ⊠ | ⊠ | ⊠ | ⊠ | ⊠ | ⊠ | ⊠ | ⊠ | ⊠ ⊠ ⊠ | | |
| 30 | 60 | 90 | 120 | 150 | 180 | 210 | 240 | 270 | 300 | 300 | |

**Pin bowler**   A player who keeps his eyes on the pins when delivering his bowl.

**Pin deck**   The area of the lane on which the ten pins are spotted.

**Pin spots**   The markings on the lane which indicate where each of the ten pins stand.

**Pit**   The area at the end of the lane into which the pins and ball fall before going into the pinspotting machine, and ball return.

**Pocket**   The 1-3 pins for a right-handed bowler or the 1-2 pins for a left-handed bowler.

**Railroad**   See **Split**.

**Return**   The name given to the track on which the ball is automatically returned to you before your next delivery.

**Roll**   The action of delivering a ball towards the pins is called a 'roll'.

*The area between the 1-3 pin is known as the 1-3 pocket. It is to that point that right-handed bowlers should aim to stand any chance of a strike. Left-handed bowlers aim at the 1-2 pocket.*

**Pocket**

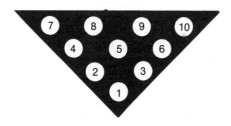

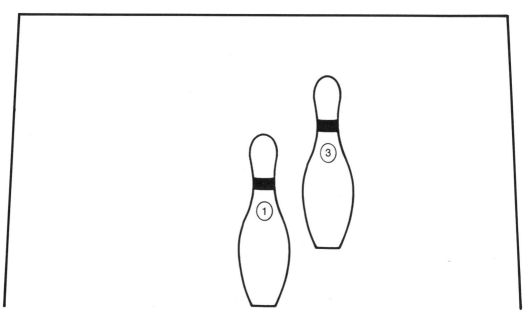

**Sandbagging**   Deliberately keeping one's score down to gain a high handicap is referred to as 'sandbagging'.

**Set up**   When all ten pins are standing on their spots, either at the commencement of a frame or if the pins are re-spotted after a miss or foul.

**Sleeper**   When one pin is left standing directly behind another pin, it is said to be a 'sleeper'. The 8 pin is a sleeper behind the 2 pin, 9 is a sleeper behind 3, and 5 is a sleeper behind 1. Spares involving sleepers are actually surprisingly easy to make, and it won't be long before you find you are proficient at them.

*This diagram shows the three 'sleepers' – the 5, 8 and 9 pins. They are called 'sleepers' because they are 'hidden' behind the 1, 2 and 3 pins respectively.*

*Sleeper*

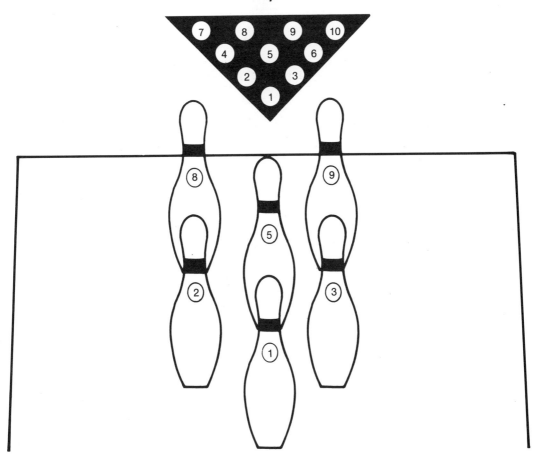

# TENPIN · BOWLING

*Sour apple split*

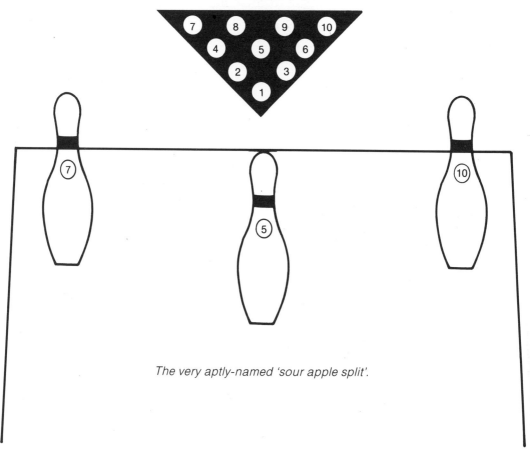

*The very aptly-named 'sour apple split'.*

**Sour apple split**   The 5-7-10 pin leave is the 'sour apple split'.

**Spare**   The knocking down of all standing pins with the second roll of the ball.

**Split**   When the headpin has been knocked down two or more pins are left after the first roll with the gap greater than the width of a ball between any two pins. Obviously a number of different splits can occur. We shall look at some, and how to deal with them, later on.

**Spot bowler**   A player who keeps his eye on the lane markers when delivering his ball, as opposed to looking at the pins.

**Strike**   The knocking down of all ten pins with your *first* roll of the ball.

*Above right: The 3-6 leave is **not** a split . . .*

*. . . but leave the 8 pin standing as well, and **now** you have a split. (Below right.)*

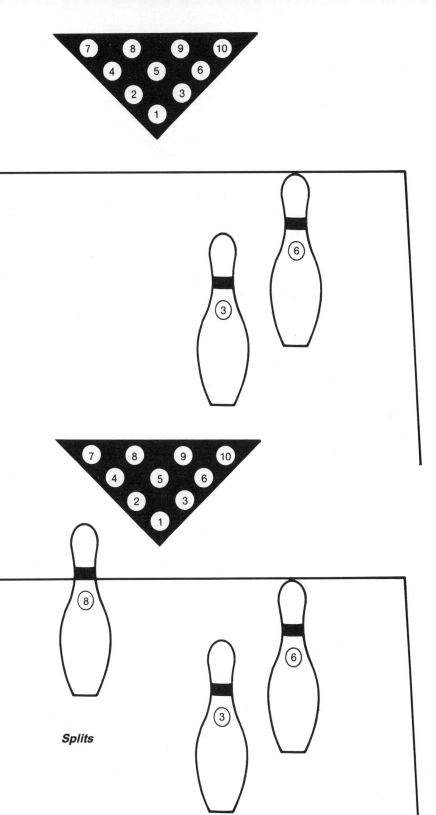

*Splits*

**Preparing for a delivery.**

# EQUIPMENT · & · TERMINOLOGY

**Strike out**  When a player finishes a game with a number of consecutive strikes he is said to have had a 'strike out'.

**Strike outs**
*In the example below the successful player has 'struck out' with five consecutive strikes.*

| 1 | 2 | 3 | 4 | 5 | 6 | 7 | 8 | 9 | 10 | Total |
|---|---|---|---|---|---|---|---|---|---|---|
| 9 ⟋ | 8 — | 8 ⏐ | ☒ | ☒ | 8 ⟋ | 7 2 | ☒ | ☒ | ☒☒☒ | |
| 18 | 26 | 35 | 63 | 83 | 100 | 109 | 139 | 169 | 199 | 199 |

**Tap**  When a pin remains standing after apparently delivering a ball good enough to warrant a strike. In such a case the number 8 pin will normally be the pin left standing for right-handed bowlers and the 9 pin for left-handers.

**Triple**  Another name for a 'turkey' (three strikes in a row).

*This common spare, involving the 1-2-7 pins, is known as the 'washout'.*

**Washout**

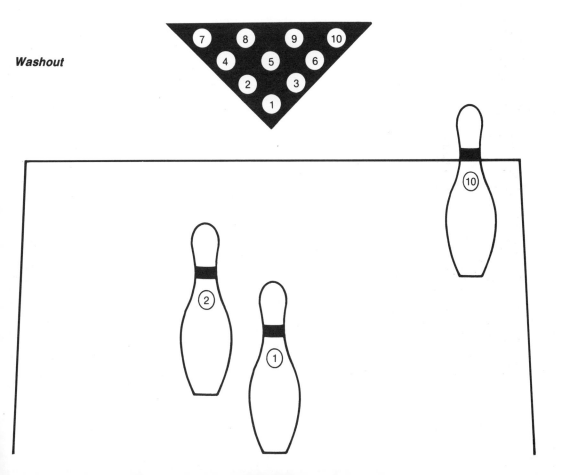

**Turkey**   Three strikes in a row from one bowler. Also known as a 'triple'.

**Washout**   Similar to a split, except the headpin is still standing. The 1-2-10 and 1-3-7 leaves are examples of the 'washout'.

**Woolworth**   The name given to the 5-10 split. Instructions on how to play a woolworth are given on page 73.

### The woolworth

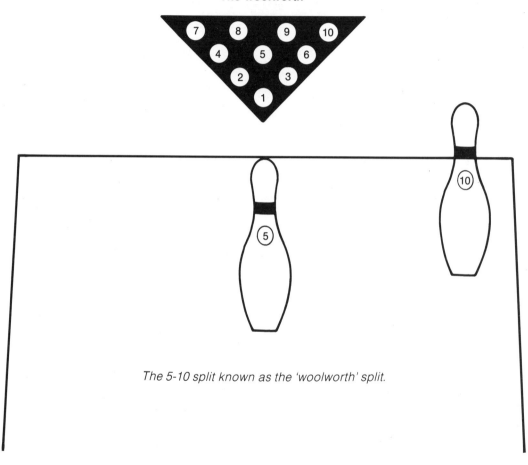

*The 5-10 split known as the 'woolworth' split.*

# THE GAME – A GUIDE

## RULES · OF · TENPIN · BOWLING

The rules of tenpin bowling are few, and simple. But the one aspect of the game that remains a mystery to many new players is the scoring system. That, too, is also simple yet many people still believe it to be complicated. As a result people will often devise their own scoring system rather than check out how to do it properly. When you play tenpin bowling you will be given a score sheet and most sheets give a brief explanation of the scoring system. However, I will explain the scoring fully in a moment. But first of all, the rules.

The object of the game is to bowl your ball down the lane and knock as many pins down as you can.

A game consists of ten frames and each frame consists of a maximum two rolls of your ball. If, however you knock all ten pins down with your first ball you have scored a strike and do not need to roll your second ball. Players take it in turns to play alternate frames.

The number of pins you score in each frame is added to your score but for making a strike and a spare (the knocking down of all the remaining pins with your second ball) you receive bonus points. In the case of a strike you score 10 for knocking down all ten pins *plus* the value of the pins scored with

your next *two* balls. For making a spare your score is 10 points *plus* the total of the pins knocked down with your *next ball*.

You have to wait until it is your turn to play your next frame before being able to establish what your bonus score is. Bonus scores are calculated as a result of pins scored in the next frame. *They are not scored as a result of being entitled to separate deliveries.*

The player with the most points at the end of the tenth frame is the winner. If you make a strike with the first ball of the tenth frame, because you need two extra balls to complete your score, you are allowed two more deliveries. If you make a spare in the final frame, you are allowed one more roll.

All the pins scored must count and no pins may be conceded.

A ball must be rolled under-arm and along the surface of the lane. It is legally delivered when it leaves the bowler's possession and crosses the foul line into the playing area of the lane.

Every ball delivered shall count unless it is declared a dead ball, in which case the pins shall be re-spotted and the player shall deliver his ball again. A ball is deemed dead if:

(a) Attention is brought to the fact that a pin

was missing from the set-up immediately after the delivery of the ball.

(b) A human pinsetter interferes with any pin or pins before they stop rolling, or before the ball reaches them.

(c) A player bowls on the wrong lane.

(d) A player bowls out of turn.

(e) A player is interfered with by a pinsetter, a fellow bowler, spectator or any moving object as the ball is being delivered. He must, before the delivery is completed, announce that he will accept the resulting pinfall or demand the re-spotting of the pins.

(f) Any pins at which a player is bowling are knocked down in any manner before the ball reaches the pins.

(g A player's ball comes into contact with any foreign object.

Just as in other sports, fouls can be committed in tenpin bowling.

When any part of your body encroaches upon or goes beyond the foul line and touches any part of the lane equipment or building (wall or pillar maybe) during or after execution of the delivery it is a foul. All pins knocked down shall not count but the ball will count towards the frame. If the foul is committed on the first ball of the frame the pins must be re-spotted and the second ball delivered at all ten pins. If all ten pins are knocked down with the second ball of a frame after a foul, the score shall count as a spare and not a strike.

An electronic eye is beamed across the lane at the foul line to indicate if your foot crosses the line. This eye is not normally switched on for casual play but is used for league matches and tournaments.

# SCORING

Scoring in tenpin bowling is NOT as complicated as people often believe. The simple rules to remember are:

(a) Your score is accumulative after each frame.

(b) The number of pins knocked down in each frame is the amount you score.

(c) You receive bonuses for strikes and spares.

    (i) For a strike you score 10 points plus the number of pins knocked down with your next two balls.

    (ii) For a spare you receive 10 points plus the number of pins knocked down with your next ball.

Let us try and make it easier by showing you some detailed examples.

First of all look at the scoresheet to see how it is designed. You will see a square representing each of the ten frames. In the top of each square are two more smaller squares, they are for entering the number of pins knocked down by each ball in a frame. The cumulative score after each frame is entered in the larger square. You will see in frame 10 that there are three small squares and not two. The extra one is to accommodate the additional ball if a strike, or spare, is obtained in the last frame.

Every pin knocked down with each ball is entered in the smaller squares but if you make a strike, spare, miss or foul then special symbols are used.

A strike is marked by an X, a spare by a /, a miss by a —, and a foul by the letter F.

Right. Now for some specific examples.

Let us start with three easy frames where no strikes or spares are obtained.

*If your foot goes over the foul line the electronic eye will activate the pinsetter and tell it you have made a foul shot.*

*A standard scorecard.*

# TENPIN · BOWLING

No. 10278

LANE: _____

GAMES: _____

| NAME | 1 | 2 | 3 | 4 | 5 | 6 | 7 | 8 | 9 | 10 | TOTAL |
|---|---|---|---|---|---|---|---|---|---|---|---|
| 1 | | | | | | | | | | | |
| 2 | | | | | | | | | | | |
| 3 | | | | | | | | | | | |
| 4 | | | | | | | | | | | |
| 5 | | | | | | | | | | | |
| 6 | | | | | | | | | | | |
| 7 | | | | | | | | | | | |
| 8 | | | | | | | | | | | |
| 9 | | | | | | | | | | | |
| 10 | | | | | | | | | | | |
| 11 | | | | | | | | | | | |
| 12 | | | | | | | | | | | |

| FRAMES | 1 | 2 | 3 | 4 | 5 | 6 | 7 | 8 | 9 | 10 | Total |
|---|---|---|---|---|---|---|---|---|---|---|---|
| | X | 7   2 | 8   – | 7 / | 8   1 | X | 8 / | X | 9   – | X   8 | |
| RUNNING TOTAL | 19 | 28 | 36 | 54 | 63 | 83 | 103 | 122 | 131 | 151 | 151 |
| EXPLANATION | 10+7+2 | 19+7+2 | 28+8 | 36+10+8 | 54+8+1 | 63+10+10 | 83+10+10 | 103+10+9 | 122+9 | 131+10+10 | |

# THE · GAME — A · GUIDE

## Frame 1

With the first ball seven pins are knocked down. The score of 7 is inserted in the first small box. In attempting to make the spare

only one pin is knocked down, then a 1 is inserted in the next box and a cumulative total of 8 for the frame written in the larger box. (See below.)

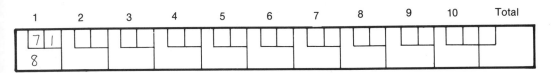

## Frame 2

Only six pins are knocked down first time and none the second time. The first box must

therefore have 6 entered in it while the adjacent box shall be marked with a —, and the cumulative total of 14 inserted.

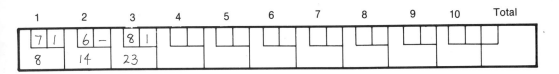

## Frame 3

The first ball yields eight pins, and the second ball one more; 8 and 1 are therefore

entered in the two smaller boxes and the cumulative total becomes 23. And so it goes, right through all ten frames.

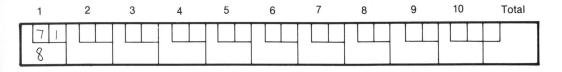

That was nice and easy wasn't it? Now let's look at three more opening frames, but this time we will introduce a spare.

## Frame 1

As before, seven pins go down first ball and

one with the second giving a frame score of 8. Mark the card in the normal way.

## Frame 2

This time the six pins knocked down with the first ball are converted into a spare by knocking down all four remaining pins. A / is marked in the second of the smaller boxes,

but you *cannot* enter any figure in the cumulative frame score because, as stated earlier, a spare is worth 10 points *plus* the value of pins knocked down with your next ball. On to frame 3 . . .

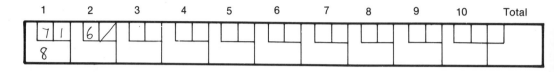

## Frame 3

Eight pins go down with your first ball, and one with the second. Right, before you enter any score in frame 3 we have frame 2 to get out of the way first.

Your score before frame 2 stood at 8; as a result of the spare in frame 2 you add 10 to

that *plus* the eight from the first ball of frame 3, which gives a total of 26. This is inserted in the frame 2 box. As a result of scoring 9 in frame 3, and with not making a spare, you can add the cumulative score in frame 3, which is now 35. Look at the card below and all should become clear!

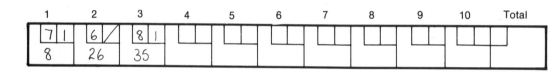

That wasn't too bad was it? Let's now go
back to the start of the three frames but this
time we will introduce strikes *and* spares.

## Frame 1

Let's say you get a strike with your first ball (well done!). You have to enter an X in the

first box but cannot enter any cumulative score because a strike is worth 10 plus the value of your next two balls.

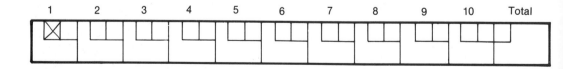

**The pinspotter replacing the pins.**

# TENPIN · BOWLING

## Frame 2

You knock down nine pins with your first ball and make the spare with your second roll. Your two boxes should therefore contain a 9 and a /. As you have now completed the two extra balls to determine your bonus for frame 1, you can go back and insert your score for the opening frame which is 10 + 9 + 1; i.e. 20. Even though you have completed frame 2 you cannot enter your score because you need to know the value of the first roll of frame 3 to establish your bonus for the spare. Had you not made the spare you could have entered your score.

| 1 | 2 | 3 | 4 | 5 | 6 | 7 | 8 | 9 | 10 | Total |
|---|---|---|---|---|---|---|---|---|----|-------|
| ⊠ | 9 / | | | | | | | | | |
| 20 | | | | | | | | | | |

## Frame 3

You score seven pins with your first ball and two with the second (what's happened to you? You started off ever so well!).

Your bonus for your spare in frame 2 is now worth 7 and the cumulative score after that frame is now 37. And after scoring 9 in frame 3 you can insert your new cumulative total, which is 46. Why not make up some scores and fill in the boxes yourself?

| 1 | 2 | 3 | 4 | 5 | 6 | 7 | 8 | 9 | 10 | Total |
|---|---|---|---|---|---|---|---|---|----|-------|
| ⊠ | 9 / | 7 2 | | | | | | | | |
| 20 | 37 | 46 | | | | | | | | |

If your opening three frames were all strikes, apart from not really having any need of this book your scorecard would look like this. You would have scored 30 points from your first frame but could not enter the scores for the next two frames because you have not rolled sufficient balls to calculate your bonus for frames 2 and 3.

| 1 | 2 | 3 | 4 | 5 | 6 | 7 | 8 | 9 | 10 | Total |
|---|---|---|---|---|---|---|---|---|----|-------|
| ⊠ | ⊠ | ⊠ | | | | | | | | |
| 30 | | | | | | | | | | |

Let us look at some more detailed examples, but this time we will look at full frames:

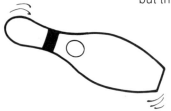

# THE · GAME – A · GUIDE

This is how you have scored in each frame:

| Frame | 1st Ball | 2nd Ball | Frame | 1st Ball | 2nd Ball | |
|-------|----------|----------|-------|----------|----------|---|
| 1 | 8 | 2 | 6 | 9 | 1 | |
| 2 | 10 | | 7 | 10 | | |
| 3 | 7 | 1 | 8 | — | 8 | |
| 4 | 10 | | 9 | 7 | 3 | |
| 5 | 10 | | 10 | 7 | 3 | 10 (3rd ball) |

This is how the scorecard would look:

| 1 | 2 | 3 | 4 | 5 | 6 | 7 | 8 | 9 | 10 | Total |
|---|---|---|---|---|---|---|---|---|---|---|
| 8 / | ⊠ | 7 1 | ⊠ | ⊠ | 9 / | ⊠ | – 8 | 7 / | 7 / ⊠ | |
| 20 | 38 | 46 | 75 | 95 | 115 | 133 | 141 | 158 | 178 | 178 |

Another but this time it is mostly strikes and spares, with the odd foul thrown in:

| Frame | 1st Ball | 2nd Ball | Frame | 1st Ball | 2nd Ball | |
|-------|----------|----------|-------|----------|----------|---|
| 1 | 10 | | 6 | F | 10 | |
| 2 | 10 | | 7 | 10 | | |
| 3 | 7 | 3 | 8 | 8 | 2 | |
| 4 | 10 | | 9 | 7 | — | |
| 5 | 10 | | 10 | 10 | 8 | 2 (3rd ball) |

And this is what the scorecard would look like:

| 1 | 2 | 3 | 4 | 5 | 6 | 7 | 8 | 9 | 10 | Total |
|---|---|---|---|---|---|---|---|---|---|---|
| ⊠ | ⊠ | 7 / | ⊠ | ⊠ | F / | ⊠ | 8 / | 7 – | ⊠ 8 / | |
| 27 | 47 | 67 | 87 | 107 | 127 | 147 | 164 | 171 | 191 | 191 |

# RULES CLINIC

**You say that all frames must be played out in full and pins cannot be conceded. Why not?**

If you are playing just for fun then it doesn't matter, apart from the fact that you will lose part of your entitled playing time. But if you are playing in a league then pins conceded will give a false reading of a player's average score which, when it came to a handicap competition, would give him an unfair advantage.

**Let's say I play in a team and have won my game with a complete frame to go. Can I deliberately foul so as to keep my average score down?**

No. You will be immediately removed from the game, or series, and stand to be severely reprimanded as to future conduct.

**What happens if I inadvertently use somebody else's ball?**

Say sorry and don't let it happen again! This happens quite often when you don't possess your own ball, but you are not penalized if you roll someone else's instead.

**Can a pin rebound from the pin deck to the side or back of the lane and knock down other pins?**

Yes, and they all count.

**Occasionally the pinsetting machine will incorrectly place a pin off its spot. What should happen in that case?**

If it is noticed before you deliver your ball then you can have the pins re-spotted correctly. If, however, it is noticed after you have made your delivery then you have to accept the resulting pinfall. This only applies on the first delivery. If a pin picked up off its spot is replaced, also off its spot, then it has to be played from where it stands on the second delivery.

**What happens if the machinery fails to remove all pins and some are left in the gutter or on the lane?**

They should be removed before the next ball is delivered.

# RULES · CLINIC

### Can a ball which enters the gutter knock pins down?

Yes it is possible, but any pins so knocked down do not count, although the ball counts as one rolled in the frame.

### Can a ball rebound from the rear cushion behind the pins and knock down any pins?

It is possible but extremely rare. However, pins knocked down by a rebounding ball do not count but the ball is deemed to have been good.

### What happens if a pin bounces off the lane, rebounds and remains standing?

This does happen occasionally. Unfortunately the pin must count as one still standing.

### What happens if a pin becomes broken during a game?

It shall be replaced by a pin of similar weight to those in the set in use.

### If two players are lining up to play on adjacent lanes, who has the right of way?

The player in the right-hand lane. This comes under the etiquette 'laws' of bowling. Other commonsense laws include not walking in front of another player who is preparing to bowl. Not collecting your ball while a player is preparing to bowl, and not taking practice swings, as these can be dangerous. Most bowling centres also lay down rules concerning smoking on the lane and taking food or drink on to them.

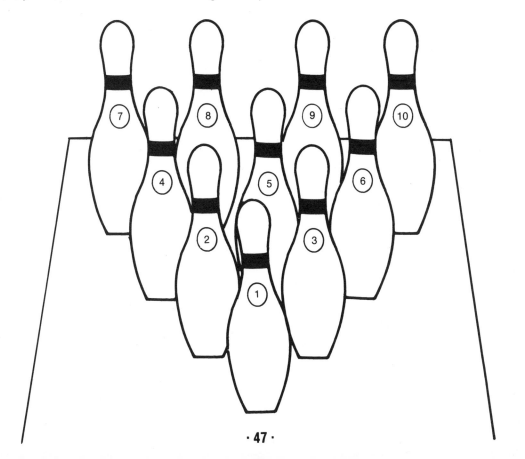

# TECHNIQUE

You may think that bowling a ball at ten pins 60ft (18·3m) away is easy. Don't be fooled, it is not. Technique is all-important in tenpin bowling. If you follow the guidelines outlined on the following pages it will help improve your game considerably. But reading a book alone is not enough, you must practise. If you don't, you'll never make a good bowler.

## CHOOSING · A · BALL

The first place to start, and perhaps the most important, is with the ball. If you have a ball that is not the right weight, or is not comfortable because the finger holes are too small, it will ruin your whole game.

To find a ball that is suited to you

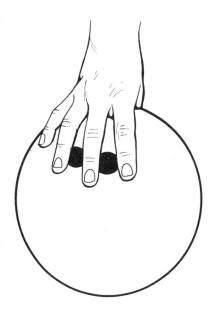

*After inserting your thumb in the hole your middle two fingers should cover the finger holes, approximately between the first joint and knuckle joint. If they do, the ball is the right size for you.*

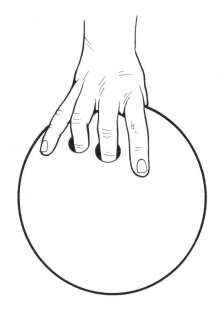

*How to hold the bowling ball.*

**A player fixes his grip and takes up his stance during the World Games.**

personally you should firstly fit your thumb in the thumb-hole. It should fit snugly but you should be able to withdraw it freely. You should then place your hand across the ball with your middle two fingers across the finger holes. The second knuckle joints should be over the middle holes. Now insert your fingers. The ball is gripped by the fingers between the first joint and the knuckle joint. If you had to move your thumb in order to get your fingers into the holes then the ball is the wrong size. If the ball is the correct size you should be able to hold it with your thumb and fingers without any

*The stance: front view.*

*The stance: side view.*

excessive strain. Try swinging the ball a couple of times. If you have difficulty holding on to the ball on the back swing then it is the wrong size.

There is normally a good selection of balls on the racks at your local bowling centre but there is no guarantee you will get the same ball on two successive visits – somebody else may be using it. If you have your own ball you don't have any such problems.

What weight ball should you choose?

As we have said earlier, a heavier ball will knock down more pins but there is no sense in using a 16lb (7·26kg) ball when you are having difficulty holding it or rolling it. Youngsters can often start with a ball as light as 8lb (3·63kg) and it is recommended in all cases that you start with a lighter ball until you have mastered the technique of bowling and then progress to a heavier ball. Women should start with a 10–12lb (4·5–5·44kg) ball and men with one 12–14lb (5·44–6·35kg).

Having now selected your ball, and feeling completely happy with it, you now need to know how to hold it . . . and how to stand.

# STANCE

You are advised to hold the ball with two hands before you start your approach. Bowling balls are heavy and if you insist on carrying them around with one hand you will soon get tired!

As you take up your stance you should be facing the pins in an upright or slightly crouching position with your weight evenly distributed between your two feet. The ball should be held in front of you approximately waist high and close to your body. Some bowlers, particularly those who use the pins as targets, prefer to hold the ball chin-high and use the ball as a sight. Wherever you hold the ball, don't hold it too far away from your body as this will cause you to lurch forward as you take your first step. Some

experienced bowlers prefer to hold the ball chest high. A ball held chest high will generate more speed at delivery but is harder to control.

The ball should be supported by your non-bowling hand which should take the bulk of the weight. If you are right-handed hold the ball slightly to the right of your body (to the left if left-handed), this way the ball

**The approach markers**

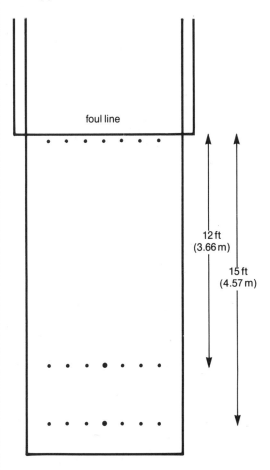

foul line

12 ft
(3.66 m)

15 ft
(4.57 m)

*It is important you use them when lining up your shots and starting your approach.*

**The correct way to hold a bowling ball.**

will naturally fall away when you start your backswing. Keep your wrist and forearm straight.

The number of steps you take in your approach to the foul line is down to personal choice but most bowlers prefer the four-step approach. It is actually three steps and a slide. Some bowlers however, use a three- or five-step approach. With the three-step approach there is a tendency to throw the ball too hard to make up for the lack of speed generated.

Lanes have markers (dots) on the approach at 12 and 15 feet (3·66 and 4·57m) from the foul line. To find out where you should start from (if using a four-step approach) you should stand with your heels against the foul line and take $4\frac{1}{2}$ normal paces forward and turn around. That is where you should start your approach from. For men it will normally be from a point between the 12 and 15 feet dots. For women it is normally on the 12-foot mark. If you want to adopt a five-step approach you find your starting position by taking $5\frac{1}{2}$ normal steps from the foul line. For men the starting position is normally close to the 15-feet dots and for women at a point between the 12 and 15-feet marks.

# THE · APPROACH & · DELIVERY

At all times during the approach and delivery, you must keep your eyes on the target which can either be the pins or the lane markers.

Right-handed bowlers start a four-step approach on their right foot and slide their left foot towards the foul line at the point of delivery.

Steps in bowling are not great lunging strides but rather a gentle shuffling of the feet along the approach area. Your feet should never actually leave the ground and

your 'run-up' should be a walk . . . not a run. Don't rush things, it won't do you any good. The most important thing to remember, however, is to walk in a straight line from your starting position to your final delivery position.

Prepare yourself mentally before each shot. Build up a picture of what you are trying to achieve. That little bit of time spent preparing your shots will pay dividends in the long term.

As you take your first step forward the ball should be gently pushed forward by the supporting (non-throwing) hand. The push forward will then enable the ball to drop freely and into the backswing position as you move your left foot forward. At the end of the third step the ball should be starting its downswing and, as you transfer your weight to the left foot ready for the final slide, the ball is brought through for the delivery. At the moment of delivery both knees should be sufficiently bent to enable you to release the ball along the lane. If they are not bent enough the ball will not be close to the lane's surface at delivery and there will be a tendency to 'drop' the ball onto the lane.

At the moment of release you will have to move the weight from the sole of your left foot on to the rubber heel of the shoe to stop you sliding over the foul line . . . I told you earlier the shoes had a specific role to play.

Always keep your bowling arm close to your body and make sure your rhythm and co-ordination are smooth. It is worth practising the push away and backswing until they become second nature.

Always let the ball travel by its own momentum into the backswing, don't try and force it higher than it needs to go. A smooth natural pendulum motion of the ball will provide the best results. Don't be tempted to speed things up.

It is important to remember that the first step is all important, for it determines the whole approach and ultimately the delivery. You can therefore see how important it is to get everything right at the beginning.

# APPROACH · & · DELIVERY

*(From left to right) Note the action of this pin bowler: in the initial stance position the ball is held very high. He is using the top of the ball as his sight between him and the pins. As he starts to bring the ball down and into the backswing position, note how he keeps his eyes on the pins.*

*As the backswing continues note how his eyes are firmly fixed on those pins and also note his thumb pointing towards the pins. The thing to note as the backswing reaches its peak is how straight the bowling arm is. As the ball is brought through before delivery note the position of the fingers and particularly the thumb – it is pointing towards its target.*

*. . . And finally, the moment of delivery. Little has changed. The arm is straight, the eyes are on the target and the thumb is pointing towards the target. Everything about that delivery was perfect.*

# TENPIN · BOWLING

## *The bowler's view*

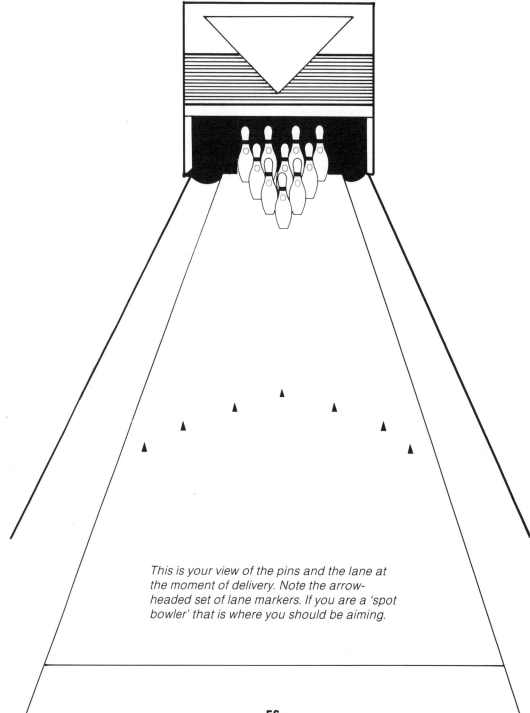

This is your view of the pins and the lane at
the moment of delivery. Note the arrow-
headed set of lane markers. If you are a 'spot
bowler' that is where you should be aiming.

# THE · DELIVERY

## & · FOLLOW · THROUGH

As you release the ball your thumb leaves its hole first followed by the fingers which give the ball finger lift – that extra power and spin at the last moment of delivery. The ball must be released smoothly and with follow through of the arm. To effect a good follow through your arm should be brought in an upwards movement so the hand is head-high. Do not allow your arm to swing across your body as this will result in your pulling the ball to one side of the lane. A good follow through will prevent jerking at delivery which will affect the path of the ball. Don't forget to keep your eyes on your target all the time. Novices often take their eyes off the target at the moment of delivery. Finally, watch the direction of the ball. You may be left with a spare and if you don't know what path your ball is taking you are going to make life much more difficult for yourself.

# WHERE · TO · AIM?

With regard to aim, you are lucky in bowling for you have two alternatives. You can either keep your eyes on the pins as you take aim, or you can aim at the lane markers (arrows) which are described on page 18. As a novice, you are advised to use the pins as a target. When you have mastered your approach and delivery, then you can start

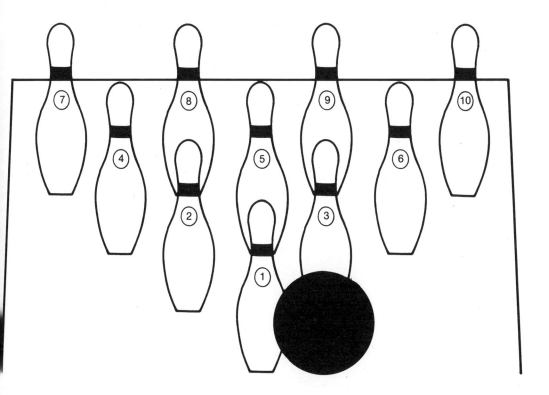

*The strike 'pocket' for the right-handed bowler.*

# TECHNIQUE

*A spot bowler*

**A perfect delivery.**

Note how she gives the ball a finger lift at the moment of delivery.

**A pin bowler**

The pin bowler has a different style from the spot bowler, but once again there is finger lift at the moment of delivery and the middle two fingers are pointing upwards.

experimenting by using the lane markers.

The initial object of bowling is to make strikes and to achieve that you must make sure your ball makes contact to the right or left of the head pin in the area known as the strike pocket. There are two strike pockets; one is between the 1 and 3 pins for right-handed bowlers and the other between the 1 and 2 pins, for left-handed bowlers. If the ball hits the pocket at the correct angle it will knock over only three or four pins but the pins will then knock each other over.

When you take up your stance you want to draw an imaginary line between the 1-3 (or 1-2) pocket and keep your eyes on it. Don't look down as you make the delivery – you will not go over the foul line if you have followed the previous instructions about your approach.

Aiming at lane markers is known as spot bowling and it is easier to hit a target close to you than one that is 60ft (18.3m) away. But spot bowling is of no use if your technique is wrong. The ball may well roll over the intended arrow but the end result may be different if the technique is wrong.

Once you have your technique right and are fully aware of the path of your ball you can start spot bowling. A good spot bowler will pick out an arrow to roll his ball over and will position himself correctly at the point of delivery to make sure his ball rolls over the designated arrow. The marker most often used by good bowlers is the second arrow from the right (second from the left for left-handed bowlers).

### Strike stance

*If you roll a straight ball then you start with your right foot between the centre dot and the one to the right of it. Your point of aim is between the middle arrow and the one to the right of it.*

*If you roll a hook then you start with your right foot on the first dot to the right and you aim to roll your ball over the second arrow from the right.*

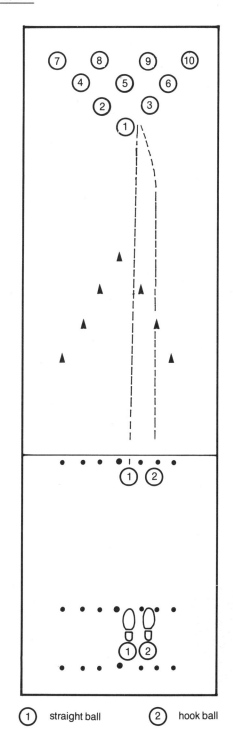

① straight ball    ② hook ball

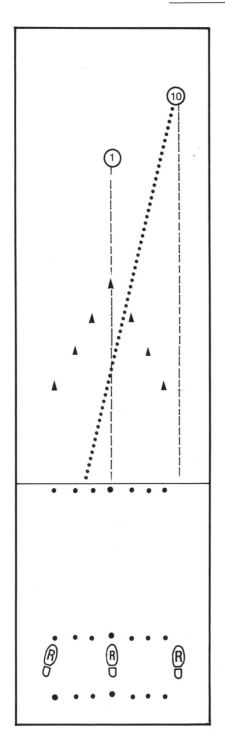

A good spot bowler will consistently bowl accurate balls, and regularly make strikes and spares.

To perfect spot bowling you should select an arrow over which you are going to roll and line that up with the 1-3 pocket (if you are right-handed). Your right shoulder should be in line with the arrow and your ball delivered over the selected marker. If you are not hitting the 1-3 pocket then you should either select another arrow or alter your starting point.

Where you aim depends on the type of ball you roll so we had better look at the various types of delivery before we go any further.

# TYPE · OF · DELIVERY

There are three basic types of delivery in bowling: the **straight** ball, the **hook** ball, and the **curve** ball.

Let's look at each type of delivery: Firstly the **straight** ball. As its name implies it travels in a straight line from the moment it leaves your hand to the point when it makes contact with a pin. To achieve the straight ball your thumb should point towards the direction you intend sending the ball and should be at the 12 o'clock position when the ball leaves your hand. As a straight ball causes less damage when entering the pin set-up (there is more chance of a straight ball being deflected) it calls for a great deal

*Positioning for the straight ball to hit the head pin full on is simple. Everything is down the middle – stance, aim and delivery. If, however, you were trying to hit the no 10 pin, everything is moved three dots (and arrows) to the right. You could, however, play a straight ball across the lane, as shown by the dotted line. This gives you more lane to play on. But you must know where your aim is, and you must turn your left foot and body to point towards the pin.*

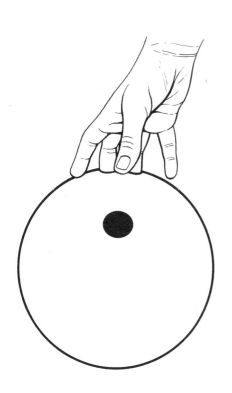

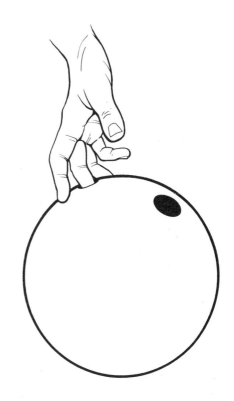

*At the moment of release of a straight ball, the thumb should be at 12 o'clock and pointing at the pins.*

*At the moment of delivery of a hook the thumb should be pointing to 11 o'clock.*

of accuracy. It is a useful ball to be able to play when attempting difficult spares and splits. To obtain a strike with a straight ball you will have to stand either to the right or left of the lane (depending upon whether you are right- or left-handed) and aim in a straight line towards the pocket.

The **hook** ball is the most common and most popular delivery. The ball travels down the right-hand side of the lane and then curves towards the pins from the left (for right-handed bowlers) and the amount of curve depends upon how fast or slow the ball is rolled and the conditions of the lane.

A hook that correctly enters the 1-3 pocket will normally be good enough to take out the 5 pin and make a strike. To deliver a hook ball the thumb needs to be at about 11 o'clock at the moment of delivery. To get your ball to hit the pocket with a hook ball you deliver it from the middle of the foul line but aim slightly to the right (for right-handed bowlers that is). With plenty of practice you will soon learn how to use the hook ball to its best advantage.

The **curve** ball is an exaggerated hook. Played with the thumb at between 9 and 10 o'clock you need strong wrists to be a

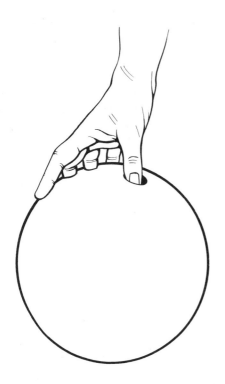

*The thumb points towards 9-10 o'clock for the curve ball.*

*The back-up ball. Note the reverse twist of the wrist.*

successful curve ball bowler. A curve ball will cause plenty of havoc as it gets among the pins but is a difficult shot to control. You want to perfect the hook before you venture on to the curve. Unlike the hook which only starts to curve as the ball slows down, the curve ball 'bends' from the moment it is delivered. To play the curve ball into the pocket you need to play from the left-hand side of the foul line and aim well to the right of the lane in order to get the curve to bring the ball into the 1-3 pocket (vice versa if you are left-handed).

There is a fourth type of delivery known as the ***back-up*** ball but this delivery is not recommended. The ball is delivered with a reverse twist of the wrist which (in the case of right-handers) sends the ball in an arced

path starting from the left of the lane towards the 1-2 pocket.

# CORRECT ·
## STARTING · POSITION

You have already learnt how far away from the foul line you stand at the start of your approach, but whereabouts do you stand in relation to the centre of the lane?

Starting from the correct position is very important but you cannot identify where you start from until you know what type of delivery and amount of curve you put on your ball.

For the purposes of identifying the correct

procedure we will assume you are right-handed and bowl a standard hook ball. Naturally, if you are left-handed all instructions should be read in reverse.

For the strike position your right foot should be in line with the dot to the right of the centre dot on the approach markings. At the point of delivery your left foot should slide towards the middle dot on the foul line markings and be facing the pins. The ball should roll over the second lane marking from the right. If you are not making the correct contact with the 1-3 pocket you should adjust your starting position by moving to the right or left accordingly. Once you have established the correct position for your type of delivery, remember it and start from the same place all the time when going for the strike.

Tenpin bowling is not a 'hit-and-miss' game. You and your ball have to be in the right place at the right time for successful results. If you follow the foregoing instructions and ally them with the correct delivery action then strikes will become a regular feature of your game.

However, even the best players do not make strikes all the time and the basis of good bowling is the ability to make spares. Don't fall into the trap of thinking that if you haven't made a strike or spare in this frame you will make it up with a couple of strikes later in the game . . . it doesn't work like that!

# MAKING · SPARES

As we have just said, making spares is the key to being a good bowler.

When attempting spares the first principle to remember is: you stand on the opposite side of the lane to where the pin is standing. This, of course, assumes you bowl a hook ball. Right-handed bowlers have difficulty making spares on the right side of the lane while left-handers have the same problem with pins standing on the left side.

Never assume that a spare will be easy to

make – they are not. Some are easier than others. The 1-2-5 spare is a lot easier than the 7-10 split but if it is that easy why didn't you hit the 1 pin in the first place?

The important point to remember about making spares is that you should be fully aware of how you are going to tackle the situation before you line yourself up to make the delivery. Nothing can be left to chance.

As there are hundreds of different possible spare combinations it is impossible to show you how to play all of them but hopefully the following examples will help you to understand how to play the more common, and the more difficult, spares and then adapt them to suit your own game or any particular spare you may find yourself faced with.

# EXAMPLES

(These examples assume that you are a right-handed bowler who bowls the hook ball.)

## The 5-pin spare

If the spare consists of the 5 pin (or 1 pin) you want to position your right foot at the dot to the right of centre. Your left foot at delivery should be on the centre dot and pointing towards the target. The ball is rolled over the second marker. In making this spare your body and shoulders must be in line with the foul line at the commencement of your approach and at the moment of delivery.

## The 2-pin spare

If the spare involves the 2 pin (or 8 pin) the right foot should be moved slightly more to the right at the commencement of your approach. But thereafter everything is the same as for the spare involving the 5 pin.

## The 4-pin spare

If the pin (or pins) left standing are on the left side of the lane you have to move your right foot further to the right at the start of

## The 5-pin spare

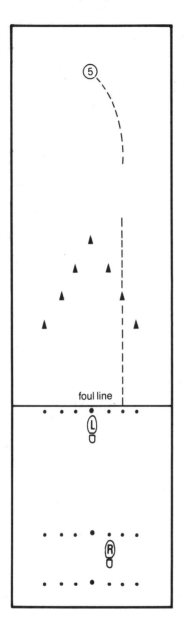

foul line

## The 2-pin spare

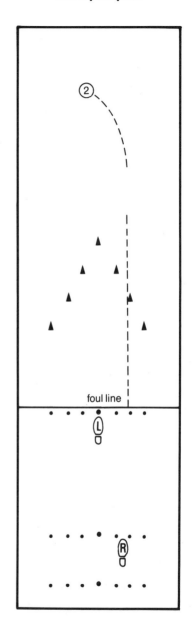

foul line

*This position is also adopted for the 1-pin spare and the following: 1-2-3-5 bucket; 1-3-10; 1-3; 1-3-6-7-10; 1-5; 5-8; 5-9 . . . and many more.*

*This position is also adopted for the 8-pin spare and the following: 1-2-4; 1-2-7; 1-2-4-7; 1-2-3; 1-2-10; 2-5; 2-4-5-8 bucket; 2-8; 4-5; 5-10 . . . plus many other combinations.*

## The 4-pin spare

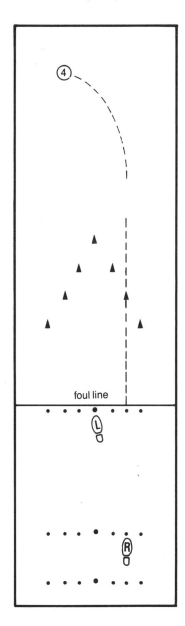

foul line

*Some other spares that can be obtained from this position are: 4-7; 4-8; 2-4; 2-9; 2-4-7-10; 2-7.*

your approach. In the case of the 4 pin being left, the right foot should align with the second dot from the right. Your left foot should still be at the centre dot on the foul line at the time of delivery but this time is slightly slanted and pointed towards the pin which will cause your body to also aim towards the pin. Once again the ball is rolled over the second arrow.

You will by now have gathered two important facts: (i) the left foot always arrives at the foul line in the centre of it and (ii) the ball is always rolled over the second marker . . . In other words, you don't change your bowling position for each shot – you move your body on the approach.

## The 7-pin spare

When the pin left standing is the 7 pin, the right foot is moved level with the outside dot. Because the left foot is pointing towards the pin at the moment of delivery your body will again be at an angle to the foul line.

## The 3-pin spare

We will now look at spares on the other side of the lane starting with the 3 pin. This time your right foot is slightly to the left of the centre dot and you start your approach with your body at a slight angle to the right. Your left foot once again is at the middle of the foul line and pointing towards the object pin. Just because you are now attempting a spare on the opposite side of the lane it doesn't mean you roll your ball in a different position, it still goes over the second arrow from the right hand gutter. The ball will curve towards the gutter but don't panic . . . it will curve back towards the pin.

## The 6-pin spare

If the spare consists of the 6 pin all that you need to alter is your right foot, which should be in line with the first dot to the left of centre, and move your body a little further to the right. The delivery is the same as that for the 3-pin spare. Don't forget, the ball still goes over the second arrow.

### The 7-pin spare

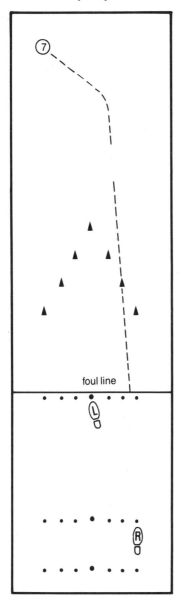

### The 3-pin spare

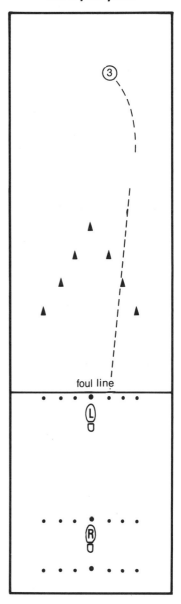

The difficult 4-7-10 split should be attempted from this position, so should the 7-10 'Bedposts', but to make this one you have to make a very thin contact with the 7 pin on the left side. The 4-10 and 4-9 splits should also be attempted from this position.

Other spares that can be attempted from this position include: 1-3; 1-3-9; 1-3-6-10; 5-6; 5-9; 5-7; 3-5-10; 1-3-6-7-10.

### The 6-pin spare

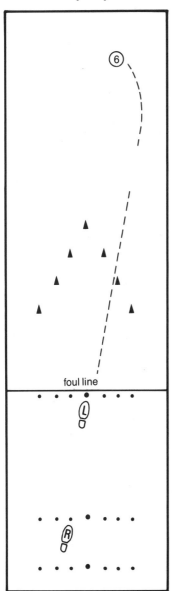

### The 10-pin spare

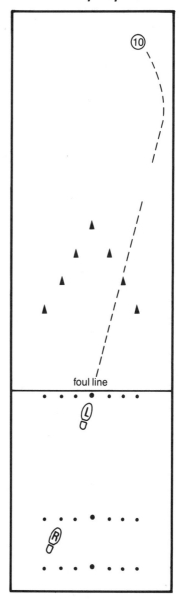

*Other spares that should be attempted from this position include: 6-9; 6-10; 3-7; 4-6-10; 7-9-10; 4-6-9-10.*

*This shot should be played when attempting the following splits: 6-7-10; 6-7-9-10; 6-8-10; 6-7; 6-8; 4-6; 4-6-7-10; 4-6-7; 4-7-8-10; 4-6-9-10. Note the direction the right foot is facing at the start of the approach.*

## The 10-pin spare

The most difficult single pin spare for the right-hander is the 10 pin. There is little room for error because the ball travels along the edge of the lane and curves in towards the pin. If it travels out too far it will fall in the gutter and if it does not travel far enough it will curve in too far and miss the pin altogether.

Unlike the 7-pin spare you do not line your right foot up with the outside dot, but with the second dot to the left of centre. However, you must turn your feet and body so they are facing well to the right of the 10 pin. Everything else thereafter is the same as before.

The examples given only explain how you make spares involving just one pin but they are the basis for making all spares. To help you further the following examples tell you which stance to adopt when playing various spares, and where to strike the pin or pins.

It is impossible to show you how to make every conceivable spare – there are just too many. But if we show you how to play the ones that are mentioned in the terminology section on pages 23–36 that will help you with most situations.

### The 2-7 baby spare

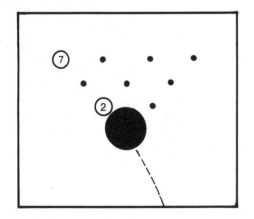

*Technique: as for the 4-pin spare.*

### The 4-6 bed posts

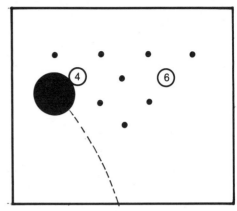

*Technique: as for the 6-pin spare. This split is virtually impossible to achieve. The 4 pin has to be hit extremely finely. It is best to play the 'percentage' game and settle for knocking one pin only down.*

### The 7-10 bed posts

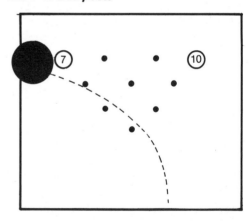

*Technique: as for the 7-pin spare. Like the 4-6 it is extremely difficult to achieve and the 'percentage' shot is often the best to play.*

**An attempt at a difficult split.**

### The 2-4-5-8 bucket

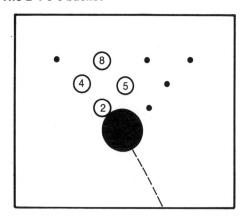

Technique: as for the 2-pin spare.

### The 4-6-7-10 big four

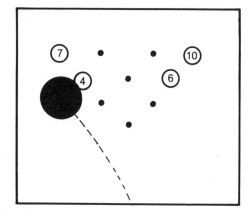

Technique: as for the 4-pin spare.

### The 1-2-4-7 clothes line

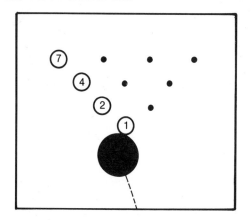

Technique: as for the 2-pin spare.

### The 2-8 sleeper

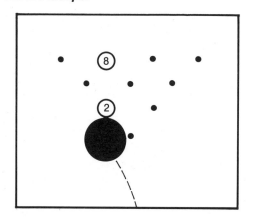

Technique: as for the 2-pin spare.

# COMMON · FAULTS

As a newcomer to bowling, you are well advised to take note of the mistakes novices tend to make.

Two of the most common faults often occur before you actually roll your first ball. The first is in selecting a pair of shoes the wrong size. You wouldn't buy an everyday pair of shoes that were too big or small, would you? So why should your bowling shoes be different? If the ones given to you by the attendant don't feel comfortable, ask him or her to change them.

The second most common fault is selecting a ball that is too heavy or the wrong size for you. On almost every visit to a bowling centre you will see novices start their

### The 5-7-10 sour apple split

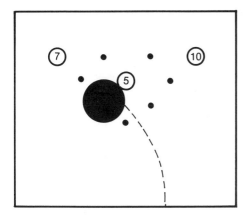

Technique: as for the 2-pin spare.

### The 5-10 Woolworth split

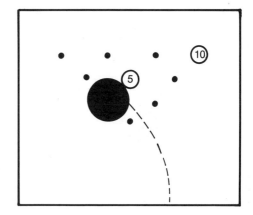

Technique: as for the 2-pin spare.

### The 1-2-10 washout

Technique: as for the 2-pin spare.

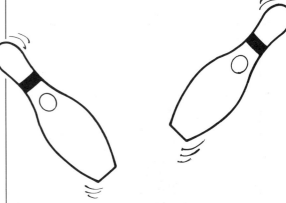

When attempting any spare don't forget that your ball is wider than the gap between two adjacent pins so it can knock both down at the same time.

run-up and go through the motions correctly (or nearly correctly), and when they get to the line just drop the ball gently on to the lane and expect it to roll the full length of the lane and knock all the pins down . . . I'm sorry to have to tell you that although sometimes they do all fall down, it is generally more to do with luck than skill or judgement.

The reason why players do this is normally because their ball has holes that are too small for them which inhibits the confidence necessary to bring the arm back and swing it fully towards the pins – they have this awful fear of not letting go of the ball and sliding down the full length of the lane! *Select a ball that is the right size and you will always bowl with confidence.*

Tight thumb or finger holes also cause the ball to be delivered too high. A failure to bend the left knee at delivery will also have the same adverse effect, known as 'lofting'. If the ball is lofted, it drops on to the lane from a height of about two feet above where it should be delivered from and it can cause damage to the lane's surface. *Make sure your thumb and fingers fit the holes and that your front knee is bent, to avoid lofting.*

If you have ever played golf you will know the temptation to hit the ball too hard. What happens if you do? Correct, it goes all over the place, the same applies to tenpin bowling . . .

Bowling is a game of delicate skill. True, the ball has to do the work, but not through brute force alone. You have to get it to work its way along the lane and into the pin formation. So, *don't be tempted to roll the ball too fast, it is simply not necessary.*

Sorry to keep mentioning golf, but in that sport the essence of good play is a good straight left arm which controls the clubhead, which in turn controls the ball, In bowling you also need a good straight bowling arm. The biggest fault among newcomers is the 'floppy' wrist. You should picture your arm, from your shoulder to your wrist, as one long pendulum which should be kept straight from the beginning of your backswing right through to the point of delivery. *Don't have a floppy wrist, and keep your bowling arm straight.*

The final fault common to novices is a failure to follow through after delivery. If you don't follow through properly it will ruin the fluent effect of the swing, which will in turn lose the control on the ball. So finally, *make sure you follow through after delivering the ball.*

You are not expected to pick up a ball and roll a 200 game the first time you play, so don't put pressure on yourself by expecting anything startling. If you score 100, be content, and build from there. The best players have off days. But they are the best players because they can recognize their faults. If you can do that and, furthermore, if you can then rectify them, you will be classed as a good player in no time.

Finally, never worry about what the players on the adjacent lane will think about your game. Nobody is going to poke fun at you if you deliver balls down the gutter. All players had to start sometime, and there cannot be a player around today who did not start out in exactly the same way as you are now. Never forget that, and you will enjoy many happy hours of tenpin bowling.

# USEFUL
# ADDRESSES

**Fédération Internationale des Quilleurs (FIQ)**
Linnustajantie 6 i 49
02940 Espoo
Finland

**British Tenpin Bowling Association (BTBA)**
19 Canterbury Avenue
Ilford
Essex, IG1 3NA
England

**American Bowling Congress (ABC)**
5301 South 76th Street
Greendale
Wisconsin 53129
USA

**Women's International Bowling Congress (WIBC)**
5301 South 76th Street
Greendale
Wisconsin, 53129
USA

**American Junior Bowling Congress (AJBC)**
5301 South 76th Street
Greendale
Wisconsin, 53129
USA

**Professional Bowlers Association of America (PBA)**
1720 Merriman Road
Akron
Ohio, 44313
USA

**Women's Professional Bowlers Association (WPBA)**
Suite 2
17 East Chestnut Street
Chicago
Illinois, 60611
USA

**Note:**

The British Tenpin Bowling Association presents badges for merit performances in matches in a BTBA sanctioned league (see below). Embroidered badges are obtainable free of charge for rolling scores of 75 in a junior game, to 275 in progressions of 25. After 275 a specially designed badge with your individual score is produced. The ultimate is the '300' badge. The BTBA issues around 10,000 badges a year, and applications for a badge have to be made on an official application form which can be obtained from the Secretary of the BTBA, whose address can be found on page 75.

# BOWLING · CENTRES
## IN · THE · UK · & · IRELAND

**Aberdeen Bowl**
George Street
Aberdeen
Scotland AB1 1HX

**Warwick Bowl**
Westley Road
Acocks Green
Birmingham B27 7UH

**Jardines Club**
Friars Square
Aylesbury, Bucks.

**Bexleyheath Bowl**
The Broadway
Bexleyheath, Kent DA6 7BN

**Bitterne Bowl**
Bitterne Road
Southampton, Hants SO2 5RS

**Cliftonville Bowl**
Ethelbert Crescent
Cliftonville
Margate, Kent

**Forum Bowl**
Longfellow Road
Coventry CV2 5HD

**Crawley Bowl**
High Street
Crawley, Sussex RG10 1BZ

**Princess Bowl**
New Road
Dagenham, Essex RM10 9LS

**ALSAA Bowl**
Dublin Airport
Dublin, Ireland

**Dundrum Bowl**
Ballinteer Road
Dundrum, Co. Dublin

**Lincoln Bowl**
Washingborough Road
Lincoln, Lincs

**Granada Bowl Belle Vue**
Hyde Road
Manchester M18 7BA

**Newcastle Bowl**
Westgate Road
Newcastle NE4 8RN

**North Harrow Bowl**
Pinner Road
North Harrow, Middx

**Norwich Club Bowl**
193c Plumstead Road
Norwich, Norfolk NR1 4AB

**Nottingham Bowl**
Barker Gate House
Belward Street
Nottingham NG1 1JZ

**Wessex Bowl**
382 Poole Road
Branksome, Poole, Dorset

**Portsmouth Bowl**
27 Arundel Street
Portsmouth, Hants. PO1 1NB

**Firth Park Bowl**
Sicey Avenue, Firth Park
Sheffield S5 6NF

**Pavilion Lanes**
The Pier
Southend on Sea
Essex SS1 2EQ

**Stevenage Bowl**
Danestrete
Stevenage, Herts.

**Stillorgan Bowl**
Stillorgan, Co. Dublin
Ireland

**Stirchley Bowl**
Pershore Rd., Stirchley
Birmingham B30 2YB

# TENPIN · BOWLING

**Murrayfield Indoor Sports Club**
Roseburn Street
Edinburgh, Scotland EH12 5PE

**Cala Gran Bowl**
Fleetwood Road
Fleetwood, Lancs. FT7 8JT

**Fraser Bowl**
4 Albany Gate
Glenrothes, Fife
Scotland KY7 5NB

**Regent Bowl**
Regent Road
Great Yarmouth
Norfolk NR30 2AH

**Airport Bowl**
Bath Road,
Harlington, Middx. UB3 5AL

**Hemel Bowl**
King Harry Street
Hemel Hempstead
Herts. HP2 4TT

**King Alfred Lanes**
Kingsway
Hove, Sussex BN3 2WW

**Hull Bowl**
Holywell/Oslo Rds.
Sutton Fields Industrial Estate
Hull, N. Humberside HU8 0XN

**Ilkeston Bowl**
Derby Road
Ilkeston, Derby DE7 5FH

**Leeds Bowl**
Merrion Centre
Leeds, Yorks. LS2

**Lewisham Bowl**
11–29 Belmont Hill
Lewisham, London SE13 5AU

**Streatham Bowl**
142 Streatham Hill
London SW2

**Sunderland Bowl**
Newcastle Road
Sunderland
Tyne & Wear SR5 1MX

**Charrington Bowl**
Kingston Road
Tolworth
Surrey KT5 9PB

**Galax Bowl**
161 Union Street
Torquay, Devon TQ1 4BX

**Granada Bowl**
Marine Promenade
Wallasey
Merseyside L45 2JS

**Walton Pier Bowl**
Walton Pier
Walton on Naze
Essex CO14 8ES

**Dolphin Bowl**
Dolphin Square
Weston-super-Mare
Avon BS23 1TU

**The Ice Bowl**
Whitley Bay
Tyne & Wear NE25 8HP

**Whitstable Bowl**
Tower Parade
Whitstable, Kent CT5 2BJ

**Phoenix Club**
Wellington Road
Wokingham, Berks. RG11 2NJ

**Wolverhampton Bowl**
41 Birmingham Road
Wolverhampton WV2 3LW

**Worthing Bowl**
Marine Parade
Worthing, Sussex BN11 3PZ

# RULES CLINIC
# INDEX

# INDEX